Original title:
The Paradise Dance

Copyright © 2025 Creative Arts Management OÜ
All rights reserved.

Author: Elias Montgomery
ISBN HARDBACK: 978-1-80581-673-7
ISBN PAPERBACK: 978-1-80581-200-5
ISBN EBOOK: 978-1-80581-673-7

Moments Wrapped in Celestial Light

In the sky, the stars do slide,
Wobbling like a wobbly ride.
Moonbeams giggle, twinkle bright,
As the clouds join in delight.

Butterflies wear polka-dot shoes,
In a parade, with silly hues.
A comet trips, falls with a laugh,
Leaving behind a sparkling path.

Jupiter juggles, Saturn spins,
While Mercury plays on violins.
Nebulas bloom in colors rare,
While space penguins dance with flair.

Cosmic chuckles fill the air,
As planets twirl, without a care.
In this ballet of starry zest,
Even aliens join in the jest.

A Journey of Unfettered Joy

Up in the air, balloons take flight,
As squirrels wear hats and kick with might.
Laughter rings from trees so tall,
As the sun plays tag with shadows small.

A frog leaps high, with no regret,
Somersaulting, he's quite the pet!
Dandelions wiggle in the breeze,
While ants dance jigs with utmost ease.

The rivers giggle, tickling stones,
While fish wear crowns of shiny bones.
The flowers hum a cheerful tune,
As bees tango beneath the moon.

In this trip of sheer delight,
Joyful pranks take flight tonight.
With a wink and a jovial grin,
The universe joins in a spin!

Flourish in Celestial Spheres

In a realm where the sun takes a bow,
The giggles of planets, oh, how they wow.
Jupiter winks with a jolly old spark,
While Mars tells jokes that light up the dark.

Stars twirl in skirts, a shimmering show,
With comets that weave and perform in a row.
Nebulas chuckle, their colors a feast,
In this wacky cosmic circus, joy's never ceased.

Gliding Through the Realm of Stars

On cosmic roller skates, we zoom and glide,
With stardust confetti that swirls by our side.
Saturn spins circles, a laugh in its ring,
While Venus dons shades, ready to swing.

Twinkling fairies poke fun at the moon,
Auditions for quirks take place very soon.
With giggles and jingles, the night unfurls,
As constellations dance with fantastic swirls.

Hallowed Grounds of Joyful Dance

In meadows of laughter, the flowers will sway,
While shadows of humor come out to play.
With daisies in tutus and sunflowers bright,
They leap with delight under soft starlight.

A garden of chuckles where gnomes tell a tale,
Of fairies and sprites on a whimsical trail.
They sip on the laughter mixed with moonbeams,
Creating a world stitched from giggly dreams.

Delight in Sylvan Embrace

In the woods where the squirrels wear tiny bows,
And trees shake their trunks with the best of their prose.
A festival bursting with humor and cheer,
Where rabbits tell secrets for all to hear.

Mushrooms tap dance, showing off their best moves,
While hedgehogs in top hats bust out some grooves.
With laughter like music, the forest rejoices,
In a merry spectacle where nature rejoices.

Spirited Steps on Dreamy Shores

On shores where laughter sings,
We twirl like playful rings,
With sand beneath our toes,
And a breeze that softly blows.

With clumsy steps we sway,
While seagulls laugh and play,
The waves join in the fun,
Underneath the bright sun.

Our shadows dance in line,
As we sip on sweet wine,
Each splash a silly cheer,
For paradise is near.

So let the rhythm flow,
As we dance to and fro,
With giggles in the air,
In this joy we gladly share.

Lightfooted Whims of Joyfulness

Bouncing like the springtime air,
We hop without a care,
Each giggle burbles bright,
As we dance into the night.

Feet tap on rainbow ground,
With silly leaps around,
Every twirl spins delight,
In the moon's playful light.

Like butterflies on the run,
We flutter, oh, what fun!
Caught in a whirlwind spree,
Our hearts dance wild and free.

So join this merry crew,
With jokes and laughter too,
In whimsy we'll parade,
In rosy dreams cascaded.

Flourish in the Radiant Night

In the glow of twinkling lights,
We whirl in silly sights,
Each step a comical jest,
As we jiggle with the best.

With stars that wink and gleam,
We dance in a joyful dream,
Twists and turns go awry,
As we spin and reach for the sky.

Laughter bubbles like a stream,
In a rhythm, we all beam,
With cupcakes in our hands,
And silly, silly bands.

So let the night unfold,
With stories sweetly told,
In this flourish of delight,
We'll jiggle through the night.

Beacons of Unfettered Joy

Like fireflies in a race,
We zoom with giddy grace,
In circles we will prance,
With each delightful chance.

Our smiles create a spark,
As we light up the dark,
With dances that surprise,
And commotion in our eyes.

We spin like autumn leaves,
In laughter, joy believes,
With every hop and cheer,
We banish every fear.

As the night rolls along,
We'll sing our silly song,
In this space of pure bliss,
No happiness amiss.

Stirrings of Lucky Melodies

A chicken in boots sings out loud,
With a jig and a twirl, oh so proud.
The cat joins the fun, in a tutu so bright,
While the dog steals the stage, barking with might.

The fish takes a leap, in a bowl on the floor,
Gliding in circles, begging for more.
A frog hops along, with a wink and a grin,
Together they giggle, let the feast begin!

Dancers Beneath the Cosmic Veil

The stars are all wearing their wacky best,
With a comet named Harold, they're having a fest.
They twirl through the night, in a glittery haze,
Galactic giggles echo, in cosmic ballet plays.

A moonbeam jumps high, wearing shades cool as ice,
While a sunbeam does splits, it's quite the surprise.
Aliens tumble, all in a daze,
As they bust out the moves in interplanetary ways.

Playful Steps in Radiant Meadows

In a meadow so lush, with colors that pop,
Bunnies are bouncing and never will stop.
The daisies are clapping, swaying in time,
With a rhythm that's silly, yet perfectly rhyme.

Grasshoppers chirp to a jazzy refrain,
While butterflies flutter, a colorful train.
A sheep joins the fray, with a skip and a hop,
They dance in the sun, oh, they'll never stop.

Relish in Joyful Reverberation

The squirrels are cooking, a nutty delight,
With acorns for props, they perform every night.
They twirl and they leap, with a squeaky appeal,
Neighbors are laughing, they can't help but feel.

A raccoon plays drums made of shiny old cans,
While the hedgehogs hum tunes, in quirky dance plans.
The party grows loud, with laughter and cheer,
In this woodland gala, the fun's always near!

Serenade of Sunlit Spirits

In a field where daisies bloom,
Silly squirrels twirl, dispelling gloom.
Bouncing bunnies join the spree,
Twirling 'round like wild dervishes, whee!

With hats of flowers on their heads,
They stumble and tumble, heeding no threads.
Chasing shadows in the warm sunlight,
Laughing loudly, what a glorious sight!

The sun plays tricks, a playful tease,
As butterflies flutter with whimsical ease.
They dance in circles, through the bright air,
Bumping into ants in their fancy flair.

Daydreams shimmer, in giggles they blend,
Back to the start, round they will send.
Under the blue, they leap and prance,
In the grand, merry, nature's romance.

A Mirage of Blissful Movement

In the shimmering heat, they sway,
A group of lizards join the fray.
With swishing tails and tiny feet,
They waddle and jiggle, what a treat!

Little frogs croak a comic tune,
Synchronized under the glowing moon.
Jumping high with a silly splash,
While crickets chirp, creating a clash.

Even the trees start to groove,
In the gentle breeze, they move and prove.
Branches twist in a light-hearted jest,
While the wind tickles all, oh what a fest!

With each ripple of the grass at play,
Nature whispers jokes in a quirky way.
As twilight falls, the laughter grows,
Under stars, the humor flows.

Choreography of Starlit Dreams

In the midnight sky, a scene unfolds,
Where sleepy owls and fireflies hold.
They gather 'round, a vibrant crew,
Flapping in rhythm, oh if they only knew!

Beneath the glow of the moonlit stage,
Each little creature finds their age.
The hedgehogs roll and the mice all prance,
With a scuffle here, oh what a dance!

A careful deer steps in, quite shy,
A twinkling sprightly look in her eye.
But soon she kicks up, joins the fun,
In this nocturnal hoedown under one sun.

The giggles echo through the trees,
As the stars watch on with flutters and teas.
In a starlit twirl, all shadows blend,
What a silly night, with joy to lend!

Echoes of a Heavenly Beats

In the dawn's light, the birds commence,
A clattering symphony, without pretense.
Every chirp and every warble bright,
Makes the sleepy critters dance in delight.

A pair of raccoons taking a stroll,
Jiggle and jive, they play their role.
With hands in pockets, or so it seems,
They're prancing around like vibrant dreams.

The flowers are swaying to the sound,
Of a hidden rhythm, all around.
Bumblebees buzz in a cheeky way,
Turning the garden to a cabaret!

As laughter fills the emerald plains,
Even the puddles join with refrains.
In a silly loop, they keep the beat,
Nature's folly is truly sweet!

Dance of the Sunlit Glade

In a glade where sunbeams play,
Squirrels twirl without delay.
Frogs wear hats as they leap high,
Chirping birds in ties fly by.

Dancing shadows chase the breeze,
Flowers giggle at the trees.
A rabbit in bright polka dots,
Jumps along and spins in spots.

Joyous whispers fill the air,
Every bumblebee's a player.
Even ants have formed a line,
Joining in with moves divine.

Nature's ball, a silly spree,
With mischief in melody.
As laughter rings, the day unfolds,
In the glade, there's fun untold.

Symphony of Lost Eden

In Eden's heart, a funny sound,
A jester's cap is twirling 'round.
Apples giggle on the vine,
As wild grapes start to dine.

Doves are wearing tiny shoes,
Doing steps with silly hues.
While serpents dance in striped attire,
Underneath a disco fire.

Laughter echoes through the trees,
While monkeys swing with greatest ease.
The playing field of nature's wit,
Where every critter takes a split!

In this land of merry cheer,
Lost Eden's charm is oh so clear.
With rhymes and giggles in the sun,
Each crack of joy's a dance begun.

Blooming Beats

Petals flutter, colors pop,
Bees in hats just cannot stop.
Dancing daisies twirl about,
While butterflies leap and shout.

Worms in boots brave the fresh ground,
Swaying to that bouncy sound.
Sunflowers lift their heads with glee,
Joining flowers in a spree.

All around, there's giggling grass,
Every blade has got some sass.
Wind chimes laugh with each swift blow,
While blooming beats create a show.

Nature's joy is so contagious,
Every move presents outrageous.
In this patch, nothing's too quaint,
Life's a fest—a vibrant paint!

Echoes of Utopia

In a land of quirky glee,
Where every elf plays hide and see.
Goblins wear their best attire,
Dancing round a fire's spire.

Wizards pop like corn in heat,
While fairies bring a funky beat.
Cotton candy clouds above,
Sprinkle fun, a place to love.

Jolly trolls with shoes askew,
Tap their toes like they always do.
With every bounce, they break the norm,
In enchantment's lively swarm.

Voices rise in joyous hum,
In this realm, there's laughter's drum.
Echoes ring, a silly vibe,
In Utopia, we all vibe.

This Elation in Midnight Skies

Under stars that wiggle and twirl,
Laughter bursts like a sparkling pearl,
Kites with smiles soaring high,
Whispers of joy in a giggling sigh.

Moonlight jokes in a playful spin,
Chasing shadows with a cheeky grin,
Twinkling lights join in the fray,
Whirling round, come what may.

A comet wearing a silly hat,
Dancing with clouds, oh imagine that!
Each twinkle hums a lighthearted tune,
As wishes drift gently 'neath the moon.

Here's to dreams that swish and sway,
In a comical, whimsical ballet,
For every chuckle and joyous sound,
Brings a sparkle to the night all around.

Woven Harmonies of Delight

In a meadow where the giggles grow,
Breezes tickle with a joyful blow,
Flowers sway with a rhythmic cheer,
As butterflies whisper jokes in your ear.

Sunbeam melodies play on repeat,
While ants march along to a silly beat,
Bees buzz tunes in perfect time,
Creating a symphony so sublime.

Frogs in hats leap with flair,
Sing "ribbit-ribbit" without a care,
Grasshoppers tap-dance on the ground,
While chuckles echo all around.

Under the sun, every creature prances,
Join in the fun, take your chances,
For laughter is woven with a clever thread,
In a world where joy never sheds.

Swaying Among the Cosmic Blossoms

Galaxies giggle in the night air,
Stars play hide and seek without a care,
Planets pirouette, spinning bright,
In the grand tapestry of light.

Nebulas twirl in colors so bold,
Tickling each other with stories untold,
Cosmic blooms sway to the breeze,
Dancing along with swaying trees.

Asteroids juggle with comets in tow,
Making the universe put on a show,
In this ballroom of mirth and glee,
Even black holes chuckle with glee.

So grab your partner under the stars,
Join the merriment, ignore the scars,
For here, among blossoms in space,
We laugh and twirl, a joyful embrace.

Flowing Through the Garden of Light

In a garden where glowbugs play,
Giggling petals parade on display,
Sun-touched laughter meets every breeze,
As nature wiggles with effortless ease.

Crickets conduct with a wink and grin,
Simmering songs that make heads spin,
As daisies tease with a playful bend,
In a space where laughter has no end.

Ribbons of light swirl in the air,
With every dance, joy floats everywhere,
The trees chuckle with leaves that sway,
In this sanctuary where shadows play.

So frolic, dear friend, through this bright sphere,
Where the echoes of cheer are always near,
For in this garden, let spirits unite,
In a whimsical waltz of pure delight.

Echoes of Luminous Euphoria

In a world of glittering beams,
Frogs wear hats and dance in teams.
The moon chuckles at our feet,
As we twirl with snacks to eat.

Bubbles pop in cheerful tunes,
While squirrels waltz beneath the moons.
Giddy giggles fill the air,
Laughter leaps without a care.

Dancing shoes made of ice cream,
Every twirl's a silly dream.
Swinging low and soaring high,
Oh, to laugh until we fly!

Glowing lights and silly moves,
Everyone has found their grooves.
In this joy, we all unite,
Bouncing, prancing, pure delight.

Tapestry of Radiant Footprints

In fields of daisies, feet go whack,
While bunnies bounce, don't look back.
We stomp in circles, leg and arm,
Spinning in a dizzy charm.

With wigs that dance like flying fish,
Each silly step grants one more wish.
Grinning at the crazy scene,
We leap like frogs on trampoline.

Crickets play a lively beat,
Our odd ballet feels so sweet.
As candy clouds provide a show,
We shimmy on the grass below.

Footprints bright as jelly beans,
Trace the laughter and the screams.
Together in this gleeful trance,
Oh what fun when we all dance!

Orb of Joyful Reverie

A glowing ball of jelly light,
Bounces round, it feels just right.
With every hop, we giggle more,
While cats join in, a furry score.

Round and round, the world does spin,
A pizza flies, and we dive in.
Chasing bubbles in the breeze,
Each one pops with jokes, oh please!

Pixies twirl in disco flair,
While grandpas dance without a care.
Grasshoppers lead in funky styles,
With every jig comes endless smiles.

Round we whirl, in joyous trance,
Mischief reigns, let's take a chance.
The moment sparkles, hearts explode,
In this whimsy, all's bestowed.

Mirthful Steps in Silver Shadows

In silver beams where shadows play,
Silly shadows steal the day.
They shimmy, they twist, they jump and jive,
Turning mundane into a hive.

With hats that wobble like a fish,
We prance and twirl, oh what a wish!
Gummy bears join the fun parade,
Underneath the fruit punch shade.

High kicks turn into epic snorts,
As ice cream drips from silly shorts.
Each flutter brings a joyful cheer,
With every giggle, we persevere.

In this part of shadow play,
Life's a dance, come join the fray.
Together in this gleeful shout,
We dance until the stars burn out.

Dance at the Edge of Infinity.

At the edge of a starry sea,
Jellyfish float, sipping tea.
They twirl and twist, a sight so grand,
While octopuses clap their hands.

Moonbeams slide on the cosmic floor,
Aliens giggle, begging for more.
With glitter trails and silly grins,
They boogie hard; let the fun begin!

Planets spin in a wobbly groove,
Unicorns stomp, totally in the mood.
Asteroids bob in a rhythmic race,
A dance-off held in outer space!

As meteorites break out in cheer,
Whirling in circles, everyone near.
In this soirée, oh what a sight,
Galactic laughter fills the night!

Whispers of Celestial Waltz

Stars twinkle with a mischievous glance,
Cosmic critters join in the dance.
Comets serve punch from glowing bowls,
While nebulae swirl with rollicking souls.

Laughter echoes through the dark skies,
As space kites fly, oh what a surprise!
Planets play tag; Venus takes lead,
Mars makes a joke, and the Sun's just freed.

Dancing dust bunnies leap in delight,
Chasing each other in weird moonlight.
Astrologers stumble, their charts run amok,
As these stellar beings make mischief and pluck!

Galactic giggles bubble and flow,
With stardust sprinkled, they twirl and glow.
In a giggling whirl, they spin round and round,
In the cosmic waltz, joy and love abound!

Veils of Elysian Rhythm

In gardens lush, where flowers sway,
Buzzy bees lead the grand ballet.
Daisies toss their heads so high,
While sunflowers wink and blink an eye.

Caterpillars groove to a leafy tune,
Swinging fast beneath the moon.
A butterfly twirls in fabulous grace,
A dance-off breaks out; it's a big embrace!

In the shade of a flickering tree,
A squirrel puffs out its chest with glee.
The rhythm flows, unsurpassed delight,
As fruit flies soar, joining the night.

With petals swirling in fragrant air,
Every critter comes, none can compare.
Laughter rings out, a joyful spree,
In this waltz of joy, all are fancy-free!

Steps Through Eden's Glow

Underneath the soft, celestial glow,
Silly bunnies hop, putting on a show.
Toadstools drum in a rhythm profound,
As they leap about, joy knows no bound.

Fireflies flicker, casting a spell,
Hopping hedgehogs dance with a yell.
The moon throws down its sparkling light,
While crickets chirp, announcing the night.

In taffeta skirts, the flowers prance,
Every bloom is longing for a chance.
With giggles and hops, they jump in place,
Nature's own festival—a merry embrace!

Through this soft Eden, laughter cascades,
As creatures celebrate in sweet, silly jades.
Come join the fun, let your spirit show,
In this dance of life, let your heart overflow!

Vagabond Spirits in Harmony

In a field of dancing shoes,
Laughter spins in vibrant hues.
A squirrel joins the merry crowd,
With chubby cheeks, he chirps out loud.

They twist beneath the cotton trees,
Bumbling clumsily, caught in the breeze.
One tripped and fell, a tumblehead,
The others giggled, 'He's found his bed!'

A picnic basket tips and spills,
As ants march in for sudden thrills.
"Who invited these guys?" they tease,
"Next time we'll keep it just to cheese!"

With silly hops and joyful rhymes,
They dance away the careless times.
A funny sight, with hats askew,
The vagabond spirits, a motley crew.

Celebration Under the Canopy of Stars

Beneath the stars, the night unfolds,
With wobbly legs and stories bold.
A raccoon leads the conga line,
With mischief brewing, oh so fine.

Cheesy tunes from tiny flutes,
While everyone's in funky suits.
They twirl and swirl, a clashing sight,
Awkward moves ignite the night.

Each person's trying hard to shine,
While bumping heads with jugs of wine.
"Oops, sorry mate!"—a friendly shout,
As laughter echoes all about.

In this wild piece of cosmic fate,
They dance on stars, a little late.
With giggles loud and hearts so free,
This celebration, just let it be!

Lingering Movements in the Mellow Light

In the glow of evening's grace,
They twirl about in a jolly race.
A cat leaps up, declares it a show,
With graceful moves that steal the glow.

At the edge, a hedgehog winks,
Joining in with clumsy drinks.
"Watch me twirl!" a voice declares,
Spinning wildly without cares.

Mellow laughter fills the air,
With mismatched steps and quirky flair.
One fellow slips, the crowd erupts,
He lands right in a bowl of cups!

As the night softly sighs away,
The lingering joy in each ballet.
A spectacle simply bursting bright,
As friendships bloom in mellow light.

Chasing Starlight and Joy

With shoes untied, they dash and weave,
Chasing sparkles, one can't believe!
In moonlight, shadows paint the scene,
As laughter flows, a joyful sheen.

The dog joins in, a playful bark,
As if to say, "Let's make a mark!"
They flip and flop like silly fish,
A recipe for crazy bliss.

A comet trails across the sky,
"Did you see that?" oh my, oh my!
But someone trips, and all is lost,
With giggles shared at the great cost.

Yet still they rise, with hearts aflame,
In pursuit of joy, no one's to blame.
Chasing starlight, wild and free,
In this funny, whimsical spree.

Rhythm of Forgotten Gardens

In the garden where the gnomes all giggle,
Flowers sway and do a wiggly wiggle.
Bumblebees buzz with a humorous tune,
While daisies sway under the watchful moon.

A cabbage patch hosts a very loud band,
Carrots play trumpets, so funny and grand.
Crickets croon funny, as they stomp and prance,
Every leaf flutters to the rhythm of chance.

Garden forks jiggle as they dig in delight,
Sunflowers grin, bringing laughter to light.
With laughter as seeds, they plant all around,
In the rhythm where joy and joy abound.

Velvet Skies and Dandelion Dreams

Under velvet skies, where dreams come alive,
Dandelions dance, in laughter, they thrive.
A balloon floats high, in a comical show,
While the stars twinkle just to say hello.

The moths hold a party in the moonlit trees,
With fireflies flickering, lighting the breeze.
Each bubble and giggle joins in the fun,
Springtime forever, never to run.

Laughter erupts with each pop and each cheer,
As dandelions wink at the world passing near.
The echo of jokes fills the soft summer air,
In this realm of mirth, we have nothing to spare.

Choreography of the Dawn

At the crack of dawn, the clowns make their stand,
With silly moves that are utterly planned.
Joyful sunflowers lean to hear the warm sound,
As the skies burst with colors, so silly and round.

The roosters compose in a funky parade,
Chickens and rabbits join in the charade.
Every step is met with giggles and grins,
While the sun yawns awake, our morning begins.

In a joyful ballet, the world takes a spin,
Nature throws cues, cuddles with a grin.
Lights flash like confetti in the bright morning sun,
Every day begins with a whimsical run.

Enchanted Spirals

In the forests where the mushrooms conspire,
Fairies perform, while the squirrels aspire.
With twirls and spins in the leafy green shade,
They dance around trees that are fully arrayed.

Dragonflies giggle as they flit to and fro,
Caught in a plot that's just for the show.
The owls turn their heads, shaking in surprise,
At the rhythmic display beneath whimsical skies.

And with each puffy cloud floating by,
The dance grows contagious as the wind whispers hi.
A circle of laughter enfolds the bright day,
In enchanted spirals, they twirl and they play.

Whirlwind of Enchantment

Around we twirl, a dizzy spree,
Spinning like leaves on a frothy sea.
Giggles erupt with each silly turn,
A dance of delight where hearts brightly burn.

With flowers in hats and socks askew,
We leap like frogs, oh yes, it's true!
Our laughter echoes through blossomed trees,
As butterflies bow to our whims and wheeze.

Clouds high above wear silly grins,
While the sun winks down as the joy begins.
In this whirlwind, we're free like birds,
Crafting our magic without any words.

So join our frolic, embrace the fun,
As shadows dance when the day is done.
In this garden where giggles abound,
Let your heart skip, lose what's profound.

Luminescent Embrace

Under the glow of a big, round moon,
We twinkle and whirl, humming a tune.
With a hop and a skip, we glide on the floor,
Making the stars giggle, wanting more.

Our feet are aglow, like lightning bugs near,
With each little trip, we all shed a tear.
Laughter cascades like a waterfall bright,
In this luminescent glow, we twirl through the night.

Chasing moonbeams and shadows that prance,
Here in this moment, we take a wild chance.
With chocolate-chip dreams and marshmallow skies,
We bounce and we bounce, till the sun starts to rise.

So let's dance in this magical light,
With funny little moves that give us delight.
In this embrace, where joy intertwines,
We're wrapped in enchantment, with twisty designs.

Steps Through Time

With footsteps that giggle and twinkle with cheer,
We leap through the ages, never a fear.
Do the cha-cha with cavemen, a jive with the kings,
With each silly step, our laughter takes wings.

From the jester's jive to the regal ballet,
Each step tells a tale in a comical way.
As time spins around us like ice cream in cones,
We boogie with tunes of forgotten old phones.

In Roman togas or disco ball sparks,
Our rhythms create timeless musical larks.
In every quick step, we find what we seek,
Joyful connections that bloom with each peek.

So here we waltz through the years with delight,
In this silly escapade, every move feels right.
Let history chuckle, let the ages smile,
As we dance through the timeline, style after style.

Uplifted in Elysium

With a hop and a skip, we're floating on air,
In a land made of giggles, without a care.
We bounce on the clouds, with cotton candy dreams,
Where laughter is sweeter than ice-cream streams.

In this charming realm, our hearts take flight,
Wobbling through wonders until we feel light.
With feathers and sparkles that sparkle and shine,
We jig and we jive, feeling ever so fine.

A whimsical dance with a ticklish breeze,
As we swirl and we twirl with remarkable ease.
Each chuckle a symphony, every smile a song,
In this space of delight, we ever belong.

So come on, my friend, let's take on this ride,
In a world of enchantment where silliness resides.
With joy ever-present and fun intertwined,
We're uplifted in laughter, past worries confined.

Blissful Shadows

In the glade where giggles bloom,
Shadows twist like giddy broom.
Dancing feet on spongy ground,
Ticklish whispers swirl around.

Squirrels wiggle, trying to prance,
Bumblebees join in the dance.
Leaves chuckle, swaying their way,
As sunbeams bounce and sway.

Mushrooms flash their colorful caps,
To join this fun-filled mishaps.
Even crickets tap their toes,
In the joy that no one knows.

Here, laughter's all the rage,
Nature's wild, a funny stage.
With joy that eases every frown,
In this merry, leafy town.

Ethereal Rhythms

Clouds do the twist in the azure sky,
While gossamer trees chuckle nearby.
Pixies ride on the back of a breeze,
Frolicking with flowers, they tease.

The sun plays peek-a-boo with delight,
Creating shadows that giggle at night.
Moonbeams shimmer, wearing bright shoes,
As nighttime dances with hues of blues.

Stars jump high, a twinkly beehive,
While frogs croak tunes that come alive.
Every ripple in the pond breaks free,
An echo of joy—just wait and see!

Nature's music, a playful sound,
Each note in the air, happiness found.
With laughter trailing through the trees,
In this waltz of life, a gentle tease.

Tranquil Tides

Waves tap dance upon the shore,
As seaweed sways, begging for more.
Seagulls squawk, joining the fun,
While sun-kissed shells bask in the sun.

Flip-flops flop in rhythmic cheer,
Bringing laughter as friends draw near.
A child tumbles, sand in their hair,
Shouts of joy fill the salty air.

The ocean whispers giggling tales,
Of fish in tuxedos and crabby gales.
Octopuses playfully hide and seek,
With little fish dancing sleek.

Under the moon, reflections gleam,
Illuminating this whimsical scene.
In the hush of night, laughter swims,
A world of joy that never dims.

Garden of Enchanted Motion

Petals pirouette in fragrant delight,
While bees buzz 'round, a merry sight.
In this garden where giggles grow,
Jokes sprout high, putting on a show.

Daisies wear hats, tulips on toes,
Jiving to tunes that no one knows.
The wind conducts with a playful wave,
Guiding leaves in the dance they crave.

Butterflies flutter, their wings a blur,
Mimicking dancers in a sweet were.
Each bloom a partner in nature's jest,
Sharing smiles, feeling truly blessed.

With every twirl, the colors collide,
Creating a canvas where joy can glide.
In this pocket of laughter and cheer,
The world's garden holds endless cheer.

Whispers of Bliss

In a garden of giggles, they sway,

With flowers in hats, what a play!

Bumblebees join with a buzz and a grin,

As laughter echoes, let the fun begin.

Tiny feet shuffle in silly rows,

Where daisies bow down, the humor flows.

Over the hills, a jolly tune plays,

As butterflies dance in their whimsical ways.

A picnic of pudding, oh what a sight,

With squirrels on stilts, a comical flight.

Kites made of jokes soar high in the air,

In this joyful land, free of all care.

Moonlit Reverie

Under the moon's shining glee,
Frogs in tuxedos jump with spree.
Crickets strum with a banjo twang,
As owls hoot in a funny slang.

A raccoon serves pie with a wink,
While stars giggle, making us think.
Night's a circus of silly sights,
In shadows, the mischief ignites.

With fireflies flickering, they prance,
In a zany, twinkling romance.
Laughter rolls like the tide's soft kiss,
In this moonlit world of absurd bliss.

Steps of Celestial Joy

Galactic beings bust out grooves,

With comets that shimmy, everyone moves.

Stars wearing sunglasses, oh what a sight,

Dancing through galaxies, pure delight.

Asteroids roll in a merry round,

To the beat of the universe, they abound.

With all of creation joining the fun,

In this cosmic bash, we're never done.

A planet plays tunes, a wise ol' thing,

While all of space sways, stars start to sing.

The constellations chuckle, winking at me,

As we twirl in this stellar jubilee.

Elysian Waltz

In fields where the gigglers all convene,

Gophers in top hats and grass so green.

They waltz in the sunshine, a funny parade,

With cookies for snacks, a grand masquerade.

Daisies are clapping, so joyous and bright,

As clouds float by, having a light fight.

A bouncy castle made of cotton candy,

With lemonade rivers, flowing and dandy.

Rabbits do flips, while squirrels juggle nuts,

And from above, a flock of ducks struts.

Each twirl and jump a melodious jest,

In this world of elation, we're truly blessed.

Traces of Whimsy in Twilight

In evening's glow, we stumble and sway,
A chorus of giggles, come join the fray.
With socks on our feet, we slip and we slide,
The moon is our spotlight, come take this ride.

We dance with the shadows, they wiggle and jive,
A chorus of crickets keeps us alive.
The trees wave their branches, they shimmy with glee,
As starlit confetti falls down like confetti.

Our feet tap the rhythm of laughter and cheer,
Each twirl unearths secrets that only we hear.
The breeze carries whispers, a sweet serenade,
As we chase the cool night like kids on parade.

So if you feel heavy, let your worries retreat,
Join us in twilight where life's bittersweet.
With each little twirl and peculiar twist,
You'll find traces of joy you cannot resist.

Prance Among the Celestial Petals

In gardens of giggles, we skip and we hop,
With daisies and dreams, we never will stop.
A twirl with the tulips, a leap with the larks,
We prance 'neath the stars, leaving rambunctious marks.

The butterflies watch as we wiggle and spin,
With petals for skirts, let the capers begin.
An impromptu disco with ladybugs near,
As stardust confetti doth sprinkle sincere.

The sun hides its face, and the moon takes its cue,
While the flowers join in with a dance, oh so new.
With giggles that ripple through shadows in flight,
Together we twinkle, all merry and bright.

So be not a wallflower; come join in the fun,
Where laughter erupts under moonbeams and sun.
Let's prance among petals, in joy let's invest,
For the whimsy of life is a colorful quest.

Luminary Waltz of the Blissful

Under the lanterns, we shuffle and spin,
With joy overflowing, let the fun begin.
A wobble here, giggles there, oh what a sight,
The night's a stage where we take flight.

With friends by our side and the stars shining bright,
We dance through the moments, our hearts feel light.
The breeze calls our names, wants to join in the game,
As laughter erupts in a whimsical fame.

Each step's a surprise, with a twist and a turn,
As the candles flicker, our hearts brightly burn.
With blunders and flutters, we become a parade,
In this luminary waltz, we'll never fade.

So if you encounter a stardusty breeze,
Let it carry you here, let your spirit be free.
In a world full of colors, we light up the dark,
Join the luminary waltz and make your own mark.

Melodic Steps in a Dreamscape

In a dreamscape of whimsy, let's dance with our dreams,
With giggles and twirls, we're bursting at the seams.
A shuffle with shadows, a jig with the light,
As we weave through the clouds, all snug and tight.

The melodies whisper like secrets to share,
While we frolic and fumble without any care.
With fluffy white bunnies that bounce to the beat,
Here, every strange step feels like a treat!

So wave goodbye to worries, let's float on the air,
With whimsical rhythms, we'll dance anywhere.
In a world of our making, let's let laughter out,
With melodic steps, we'll dance all about.

Keep your heart wide open, let the fun prompt your feet,
In this dreamscape of joy, life's a dancing sweet.
It's a party of giggles, a playful embrace,
Join in the frolicking, jump into space!

Twirls in a Golden Field

In fields of gold we spin and sway,
With buzzards judging from afar,
A tumble here, a bumble there,
Oh look, we've twisted like a jar!

The sunbeam tickles, laughter spills,
As daisies dance beneath our toes,
With silly moves and joyous thrills,
It's hard to keep from striking poses!

We leap and trip, then try a twist,
The flowers cheer, they know our jams,
While bees confuse our happy mist,
And join the dance—those little clams!

So hold my hand, we'll spin around,
In golden waves, we'll lose our minds,
From giggles echoing, there's no sound,
But butterflies, with flapping grinds!

Serenade of Sweet Escape

Beneath the trees we plot and scheme,
A secret place where laughter breeds,
With twists and skips, it's quite a dream,
A bubbling brook that giggles, leads.

We leap like frogs, with not a care,
And slide on mud like nose to tail,
In this sweet spot, our burdens bare,
As squirrels join in—what a tale!

A serenade of goofy moves,
As shadows dance on grassy floors,
While nature smiles, and groove improves,
We'll kick our shoes and mend our sores!

So here we laugh in wild retreat,
With every slip and sudden twirl,
We find our bliss on these warm sheets,
Of earthy joy, and little whirl!

Celestial Choreography

We swing beneath a crazy sky,
A cosmic stage where stars collide,
With twinkling jokes and giggles high,
Each step, a dance—no need to hide!

In gravity's grip, we spin and swoon,
With meteors whoop and comets boo,
As aliens clap to our silly tune,
In costumes made of silver glue!

Planets wobble in disbelief,
While we perform our joyful stunts,
The moons are watching, can't find grief,
They join in, with cosmic grunts!

Our galactic dance, a funny show,
With spirals bright, we prance and loop,
In this vast space where dreams can grow,
We laugh till stars all join our troop!

Mirage of Delight

In the heat of sun where shadows play,
We jiggle on sand with glee and cheer,
A mirage forms, it leads away,
But first, let's twirl and spin right here!

With every step, the grains do fly,
Our footprints dance a wobbly trail,
The laughter echoes, oh my, oh my,
As we trip on shells and tip the scale!

A surfboard here, a tumble there,
As seaweed sways in harmony,
We paddle on air with salty hair,
Imagining mermaids' company!

So raise your cups of coconut bliss,
Let's toast our jig on this wild night,
With giggles that feel like sandy kiss,
In this mirage, we find delight!

Spirited Revelry in Starlit Halls

In starlit halls, we gather round,
With hats askew and laughter bound.
A twist, a twirl, a silly spin,
Bumping elbows, where to begin?

The moon winks down, it knows our name,
We trip and tumble, it's all a game.
With giggles loud, and shoes untied,
We sway and swerve, our arms wide-eyed.

A dance with shadows, we waltz on air,
The stars are chuckling, it's only fair.
A tea party gone wildly wrong,
Yet in this folly, we find our song.

Oh, what a sight, our jigs, our prance,
With wobbly legs, we dare to chance.
A spirit of mischief, light as a feather,
In these starlit halls, we dance together.

The Garden of Wondrous Steps

Amid the blooms of colors bright,
We shuffle feet in sheer delight.
With bees that buzz and birds that chirp,
We frolic, hop, and sometimes slurp.

The daisies giggle, the roses sway,
As we lose our shoes and dance away.
Our shadows leap, they skip and jolt,
In this garden, we twirl and dolt.

A butterfly flutters, we wave hello,
While tripping over roots below.
Laughter echoes from each petal,
In wild step, we happily settle.

With every stomp and silly glide,
The flowers cheer, take it in stride.
In this patch of wonder, we take a chance,
For every misstep is part of the dance.

Dance of Serendipitous Sounds

Tune in to the whir of playful birds,
While we twaddle, undisturbed.
With each plucky note and silly sound,
We spin like tops, our joys abound.

The frogs groan funk, the crickets croon,
As we sway beneath a slivered moon.
Sammy's hat flies, a flyaway feat,
While wiggly toes find the beat.

Hearts light with rhythm, we prance and flirt,
In this sprawling yard, we laugh and spurt.
A serenade of laughter from each fell,
In this tangled, ticklish musical swell.

Forget the rules, we're free to roam,
Every silly shuffle finds its home.
With the pulse of joy and silly sounds,
We dance our glee on the merry grounds.

Ecstasy Beneath the Cosmic Canopy

Under cosmic lights, we skip and sway,
With silly hats and bright display.
The stars are our partners, laughing in time,
As we jig a jig, a whimsical rhyme.

Galactic giggles echo so bright,
In a sea of stardust, pure delight.
With planets beating, our steps collide,
In this wild night, we cannot hide.

Gravity's teasing, we float and glide,
Like dandelion seeds on a whimsical ride.
Throw your worries, chuck 'em away,
For tonight's our night; let's dance and play!

A universe of laughter, we claim our space,
In the cosmos, we find our grace.
Twirl and whirl beneath skies so vast,
With each goofy step, our spirits are cast.

Luminescent Grooves of Bliss

Under twinkling lights so bright,
Dancing critters take to flight.
Hopping here and twirling there,
Even squirrels stop to stare.

With banana peels, they slide,
A conga line they're trying to hide.
Jumping jigs and silly grins,
Watch out for those acorn spins!

The moonlight glimmers on their shoes,
While laughter echoes through the hues.
A ticklish breeze with jammed guitars,
That's how you groove beneath the stars!

In this garden of giggles and cheer,
Every gopher is a volunteer.
As they salsa on the mushrooms bright,
Mirthful mischief lights up the night!

Dance of the Celestial Garden

Upon a bed of petals soft,
The chubby bumblebees take off.
With wiggly bugs doing the twist,
Dancing herbs just can't be missed!

A rabbit leads the merry tune,
With hops that make the flowers swoon.
Pansies giggle in the breeze,
Sunflowers sway with utmost ease.

Dandelions float like fluffy balls,
While crickets play their magic calls.
The stars are wrapped in laughter's glow,
As fireflies join the big show!

Grasshoppers leap and twist about,
While frogs croak loud, there's never doubt.
This enchanting garden holds the key,
To the most whimsical jubilee!

Symphony of the Ethereal

A symphony of giggles forms,
As beetles dance through endless swarms.
With clumsy hops and cheeky flair,
Squeaks and chirps fill up the air.

Moonlit melodies, oh so sweet,
Swaying petals find their beat.
Slimy snails with shell percussion,
Join the fun in grand discussion.

A serenade of wobbly tunes,
Dancing snippet-jigs with raccoons.
Every critter joins the fare,
In this concert without a care!

Juggling fireflies with glee and grace,
Whirlwinds of laughter fill the space.
In this realm of whimsy sublime,
Even clocks forget the time!

A Ballet of Enchanted Moments

In a meadow, magical and bright,
A ballet unfurls beneath moonlight.
Bouncing bunnies don tutus fine,
As dragonflies sip the dandelion wine.

The frogs are leaping in grand plies,
While twirling leaves whisper soft sighs.
Swirling petals dance and flit,
This is where joy and laughter fit.

With each pirouette, sparks fly high,
Catnip curtains wave goodbye!
The earth shakes with a gentle sound,
As every whimsy spins around.

It's a waltz of whimsy and delight,
Infernal giggles fill the night.
Fairy tales in every twirl,
As magic in our hearts will swirl!

The Waltz of Infinite Smiles

With grins so wide, like funny pies,
We twirl and spin beneath the skies.
Our feet collide, what a pure delight,
As laughter erupts, all through the night.

Each swaying partner, a silly clown,
Twirling joyfully, upside down.
We stomp and hop in a jolly parade,
With giggles and wiggles, our plans are laid.

Chasing our shadows, we leap with glee,
Tangled together like vines from a tree.
A whirl of colors, a splash of cheer,
This merry dance, we hold so dear.

Every jig we take, a bright surprise,
As foolish steps lead to joyous highs.
We bow and laugh, our hearts take flight,
In this waltz of smiles, we find our light.

Celestial Friendships in Motion

Up in the sky, our friendship floats,
We dance with stars and funny goats.
With twinkling shines, we leap and bounce,
As cosmic giggles make our hearts pounce.

Each step we take, a cosmic bloop,
Spinning round in a galactic loop.
Planetary pals in a silly chase,
Floating and twirling in endless space.

Asteroids chuckle as we collide,
With every tumble, our joy won't hide.
Through rings of Saturn, we swirl and play,
In this starry whirl, we find our way.

With lunar hops and a comet's jump,
We lighten up like a cosmic pump.
In this dance of friends, we're filled with cheer,
As we waltz through the night, with all we hold dear.

Ethereal Steps on a Silver Path

On paths of silver, with shoes of joy,
We skip along, both girl and boy.
With a hop and a skip, we twirl around,
Making merry music, the sweetest sound.

Floating high on a bubble of fun,
Every step feels like it's just begun.
Silly dances under a moonlit glow,
As we laugh and twaddle, come on, let's go!

Each echoing giggle leaves us aglow,
As we jive with the breeze, taking it slow.
Fanciful meetings upon this bright trail,
With each silly move, we giggle and sail.

Together we form our own goofy crew,
Dancing in rhythm, just me and you.
With joy overflowing, here's our sweet path,
Ethereal steps that bring forth the laugh!

Dance of the Blissful Spirits

In a realm of glee, where spirits roam,
We prance and jig, we make it our home.
With each little twirl, our laughter flies,
As joyfulness spreads under starlit skies.

Flickering lights, in the moon's embrace,
We rattle and roll, an ecstatic race.
Spirits embracing with vibrant flair,
In this funny dance, we shed every care.

With tiptoes light and hearts so free,
We sway together like branches of a tree.
In this frolicsome ballet of delight,
Our blissful dance radiates through the night.

Flipping and flopping in glorious glee,
We dance as one, just you and me.
In this spirit whirl, we never feel blue,
For laughter and joy make our dreams come true.

Enchanted Musings in the Moonlight

In the glow of night, they prance,
Glimmers of joy in a silly stance.
With twirls and giggles, they sway,
Chasing shadows that play away.

Stars wink like they know the song,
While frogs join in, hopping along.
The moon, a grin, beams from above,
As crickets chirp a tune of love.

Twinkling lights mimic the feet,
Dancing flames make the night sweet.
With every beat, laughter starts,
Swinging round, they outsmart hearts.

In a whirl of colors, they spin,
Each silly move, a joyful win.
Echoes of fun fill the night air,
A whimsical charm, beyond compare.

A Festival of Ethereal Steps

Gather the night for a festive spree,
Where jellybeans frolic with glee.
Marshmallow clouds float above,
While gumdrops rain down with love.

Lollipops twirl in the moon's shine,
Candy canes dance, feeling fine.
Silly hats bob on every head,
As laughter echoes where dreams are fed.

With each goofy twirl, smiles grow,
As confetti sparks in a colorful flow.
Footprints of magic fill the ground,
In this sweet circus where fun is found.

A parade of bliss sways to the beat,
Tickling toes in a sugary treat.
Grab a partner, spin around wide,
In this funny land, let joy be your guide.

Rhythms of the Seraphim

Heavenly choirs bring a comical cheer,
As clumsy angels lose track of their gear.
With feathered wings flapping askew,
They trip on clouds, but giggles ensue.

In a syncopated beat, they fly,
Where halos spin, and shoe bows tie.
Their hums and giggles blend in the air,
A frolicsome song, beyond compare.

Juggling moonbeams, they toss with flair,
Tickling the stars with a playful stare.
In a heavenly jig, they stomp and shake,
Creating a rhythm that makes hearts quake.

With clouds as cushions, their dance unfolds,
Stories of joy in laughter retold.
In this curious space, where humor's the norm,
The seraphim show us that fun can be warm.

Twirling in the Meadow of Joy

In a meadow where daisies sway,
Little feet dance in a quirky display.
Bumblebees buzz with a silly tune,
While sunflowers nod to the afternoon.

With each spin, the laughter does bloom,
As butterflies flutter, dispelling the gloom.
Giggles burst forth like springtime flowers,
Adding joy to the gentle hours.

The breeze carries whispers of cheer,
As frolicking figures draw near.
Twirling and bouncing to nature's beat,
As everybody joins in, making life sweet.

With sprawled-out laughter, they gather round,
Creating a circle where joy is found.
In this meadow, where spirits take flight,
Life is a dance full of delight.

Splashing Joy Through Dreamy Landscapes

In fields where flowers wink and sway,
Two frogs in tutus play all day.
With each leap, they cause a splash,
As butterflies join in with a dash.

Clouds giggle down with raindrop cheers,
They make it rain candy, oh dear!
Marshmallow trees bounce with delight,
While squirrels twirl in the morning light.

The sun wears shades, a funky grin,
As the bunnies join in for the win.
They hop to the beat of a silly tune,
Dancing to the rhythm 'neath the moon.

So come, bring your giggles, bring your fun,
In this playful land, we all are one.
With splashes of joy, we'll whirl around,
In a world where laughter is truly found.

Dance of the Infinite Beams

A kite with legs does a jig on high,
As the sun showers beams from the sky.
Rabbits wear hats and twirl with flair,
With a bounce that's impossible not to share.

The grass is alive with a glowing thrum,
As ants breakdance, adding to the fun.
With jellybean confetti drifting down,
They shake up the earth with a hilarious sound.

Jumping jack squirrels wear shades so cool,
While turtles try not to trip, oh what a fool!
The crickets play tunes on a banjo,
As the dancefloor lights up with a vibrant glow.

With swings of joy, all creatures prance,
Under a sky of sparkling chance.
In this whimsical land, let's sway and glide,
Where laughter and light forever abide.

The Exuberance of Glistening Angels

Dancing on clouds with a giggle so bright,
Angels in pajamas, oh what a sight!
With twinkling toes and a shimmy so grand,
They spin through the air, hand in hand.

Feathers and sparkles rain all around,
As they leap over rainbows, joy is found.
Glowing like stars in a silly parade,
They tickle the moon's face, unafraid.

Juggling sweet dreams in a wild ballet,
As their laughter echoes, "Don't slip, hooray!"
With glimmering wings and a whooshy slide,
In this cheerful realm, we all take pride.

So join in the fun as they flit and fly,
With giggles that dance and never say goodbye.
In this sparkling cosmos, we all belong,
Where cheerfulness sings a perpetual song.

A Celebration of Ethereal Bliss

An octopus wears a floral crown,
As jellyfish waltz in the deep sea gown.
They swirl and twirl in a luminous trance,
Creating bubbles that giggle and dance.

With dolphins that whistle a bubbly tune,
And crabs doing cha-chas beneath the moon.
The fish throw a party with snacks galore,
Chasing currents, they dash to the shore.

Seashells clap as they tap their toes,
And a sea turtle moonwalks, goodness knows!
A frothy fiesta where joy has no end,
With laughter and bubbles, around every bend.

So let's float along, in the tide's sweet flow,
Where smiles are bright, and friendships grow.
In this whimsical ocean, so full of glee,
Our hearts dance freely, forever carefree.

Feet on Ethereal Ground

In shoes too tight, we prance around,
With wobbly steps on feathered ground.
We lift our toes, we spin with glee,
Dancing like moths, so wild and free.

Our feet, they glide, they trip, they slide,
In this strange place, we cannot hide.
With giggles bursting, we lose the beat,
Two left feet, still can't be beat!

The clouds above, they shake and tease,
As we unleash our silly freeze.
A twirl, a jump, then off we go,
Floating lightly in a silly show.

With every stumble, we start to sing,
What fun it is, this crazy fling!
So here we dance, our laughter loud,
Together we're a joyful crowd!

Harmony in the Meadow

In fields of green, we gather near,
With whistles, honks, and tunes unclear.
The daisies sway, they join the song,
While we keep dancing all night long.

A sheep joins in, with a leap and bound,
In woolly fluff, it twirls around.
We kick our heels and slide with glee,
Creating joy, just you and me.

The sun dips low, we see the stars,
Each twist a wish, this night is ours.
Spinning wild, we crash and laugh,
In every tumble, there's a photograph.

The crickets chirp, they steal the show,
Our clumsy moves make spirits glow.
In harmony, we make quite a scene,
In this meadow where we dance, carefree and keen!

Seraphic Sway

With halos askew, we float about,
In garments bright, we twist and shout.
The angels giggle, their wings a-flap,
As we glide by in a zany zap.

They lift their legs, but one trips high,
As feathers scatter through the sky.
In this divine disco, we lose our grace,
Yet wear big smiles upon each face.

A whiff of clouds, we inhale delight,
We spin and hop, oh what a sight!
With silly poses and jolly tunes,
We paint the air with laughter and swoons.

Our joyful jig makes heaven sway,
As giggly glimmers light the way.
In seraphic cheer, we're oh-so-bold,
Creating memories, bright stories told!

Ecstasy Under Starlight

Beneath a sky of twinkling dreams,
We prance and skip in silly themes.
With funky moves, we can't be tame,
In the magic fog, we play our game.

A splash of laughter, a dash of fun,
We twirl like whirlwinds, oh what a run!
The moonbeam sparkles upon our heads,
As we shake and shimmy on colorful beds.

Stars wink playfully, they cheer us on,
While we dance 'til the break of dawn.
Our feet in rhythm, our hearts so light,
In a cosmic jig that feels just right.

With every flip, we touch the skies,
Our giggles echo, as the night flies.
In ecstasy, we spin and sway,
Savoring this blissful, starry ballet!

Harmonics of a Blissful Heritage

In a field of giggles, they prance so bright,
Banjos and trumpets in the warm sunlight.
With shoes that squeak and hats that flop,
   They revel in rhythm, they never stop.

With every step, a shoe might fly,
Oh, where's it landed? Well, my oh my!
Laughter erupts as they chase it down,
   A comedy show in a sleepy town.

Jokes exchanged like candy treats,
Every dancer can't help but meet.
With twirls and twists, what a sight,
   A carnival of joy, pure delight.

At dusk they gather, spirits high,
Tales of the day bring a tear to the eye.
From pratfalls to puns, the night is young,
In their harmonic dance, the world is spun.

A Floating Journey of Joy

Balloons tied to feet, bobbing in air,
Skipping on clouds without a care.
They giggle and sway, a sight to behold,
Floating through laughter, a tale retold.

With whimsies of fancies and bubbles of song,
The air is sweet, nothing feels wrong.
A jellybean tide rolls in from the sea,
They dive through the waves, oh what glee!

Every splash is a chuckle, every plop's a cheer,
They dodge the waves with no hint of fear.
As they float on dreams, the sun dips low,
In a whirlpool of giggles, they steal the show.

With pumpkins as boats, they sail on the breeze,
Chasing the starlight, doing as they please.
A journey through nonsense, a radiant flight,
The world's just a chuckle, and everything's right.

The Joyride in Forgotten Gardens

In gardens of whimsy, they zip and zoom,
Over the daisies, and under the gloom.
With laughter as fuel, they're racing on by,
Oh, what a ride as the butterflies fly!

Lemonade rivers, chocolate trees,
They sip on the breeze with sugar-sweet ease.
A merry-go-round with squirrels and glee,
In this patch of laughter, they're wild and free.

The flowers are dancing, the weeds crack a joke,
A tumble of joy, where not a soul's croak.
With polka dot pants and wigs flying high,
They twirl and they skip, oh me, oh my!

As twilight falls, the stars lend a hand,
To this ride of silliness, in this world so grand.
With each little giggle, the garden's alive,
They'll ride on forever, where magic will thrive.

Performers in the Realm of Light

Under the spotlight, they prance and play,
With juggling pies and a clown on display.
A skip and a hop, a roll on their back,
The zany parade is a joyful knack.

With sparkles and giggles, the shadows sway,
A chortle and cheer at the end of the day.
Dancers in bubbles, a sight to behold,
This whimsical show never gets old.

From juggling frogs to a dancing cat,
Every odd act brings joy; imagine that!
With tickles of laughter running through the crowd,
In this realm of light, they dance proud.

As stars start to twinkle, they wrap up the night,
With one final bow, oh what a delight!
In a curtain of giggles, they take their leave,
In a world full of wonder, there's more to achieve.

www.ingramcontent.com/pod-product-compliance
Lightning Source LLC
Chambersburg PA
CBHW072223070526
44585CB00015B/1472